ANIMALS IN WINTER

P9-CEZ-114

ANIMALS IN WINTER

By Henrietta Bancroft and Richard G. Van Gelder

Illustrated by Gaetano di Palma

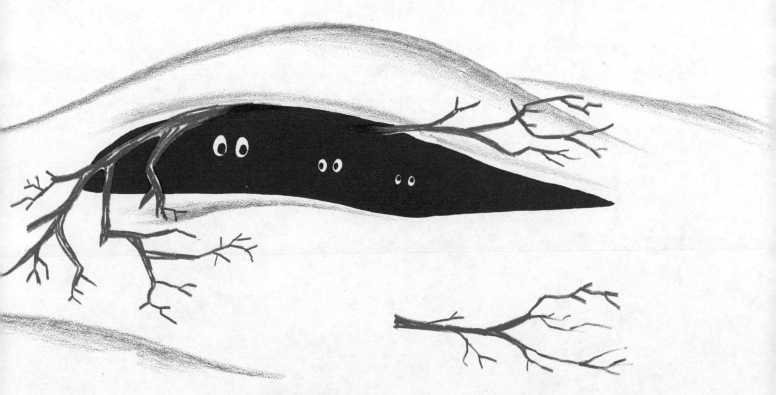

SCHOLASTIC INC.
New York Toronto London Auckland Sydney

No part of this publication may be reproduced in whole or in part, or stored in a retrieval system, or transmitted in any form or by any means, electronic, mechanical, photocopying, recording, or otherwise, without written permission of the publisher. For information regarding permission, write to Thomas Y. Crowell Company, 10 East 53 Street, New York, NY 10022.

ISBN 0-590-01321-1

Copyright © 1963 by Henrietta Bancroft and Richard G. Van Gelder. Illustrations copyright © 1963 by Gaetano di Palma. All rights reserved. This edition is published by Scholastic Inc., 730 Broadway, New York, NY 10003, by arrangement with Thomas Y. Crowell Company.

16 15 14 13 12 11 10 9 8   1/9

Printed in the U.S.A.   08

ANIMALS IN WINTER

The days grow short.
The nights grow long.
It is getting colder.
Winter is coming.

Leaves have fallen from the trees.

There are no berries on the bushes.

Insects are gone.

The grass is dead and brown.

Birds and other animals are getting ready for winter.

Some of the birds will go south.

Bluebirds and orioles go toward the south.

They go where it is warm.

They go where it is sunny and there is food for them
to eat.

Many butterflies go south.
That is what the Monarch butterflies do.
They gather in a tree by the hundreds
    before cold weather comes.
They stay in the tree all night.
In the morning, they fly away.

Many bats fly south, too.
But some bats stay in the north all winter.
When the weather gets cold, they go to a cave.

There is no wind or snow in the cave.
The bats sleep there all winter.
They do not eat.
    They live on fat stored inside them.
    They do not move.
    They hardly breathe.
    They sleep, sleep, sleep.
    They hibernate.

Bats and woodchucks hibernate.
They do this so they can live in the winter
    when they cannot find food.

Here is a woodchuck.
Maybe you call him a groundhog
    or a marmot.
He gets ready for winter, too.

When fall comes, he eats, and eats, and eats.

He eats grass, twigs, and leaves.

He grows fat.

When it gets cold, the woodchuck crawls into his
    long tunnel and goes to sleep.

He hibernates.

Does he sleep for a day?

Longer than that.

Does he sleep for a week?

Longer than that.

A month?

Even longer!

A woodchuck can sleep as long as four months!!!

The woodchuck seems hardly alive.
He breathes very slowly.
His heart beats slowly, slowly, slowly.
He sleeps, sleeps, sleeps.

When winter is over, he wakes up.
He crawls out of the long tunnel. He is weak.
The woodchuck eats what food he can find.
There is not much, for plants have
   just started to grow.

Some animals do not have to hibernate.

They gather food and save it for the winter.

That is what a pika does.

A pika looks like a chipmunk in some ways, but he is
bigger.

He lives in high mountains where winters are long
and cold.

Pikas eat grass.

In summer, they cut more grass than they can eat.
They spread the grass on flat stones.
The hot sun dries it.

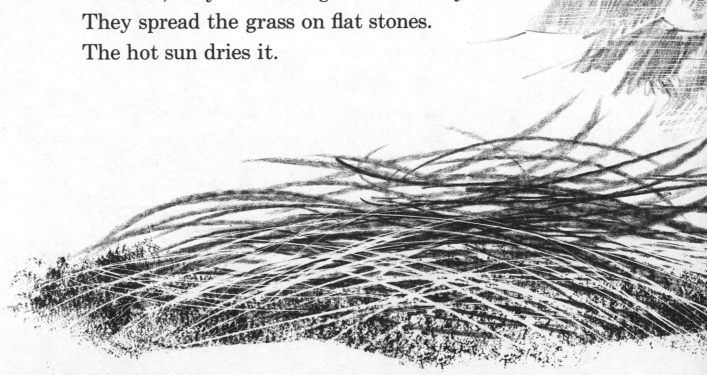

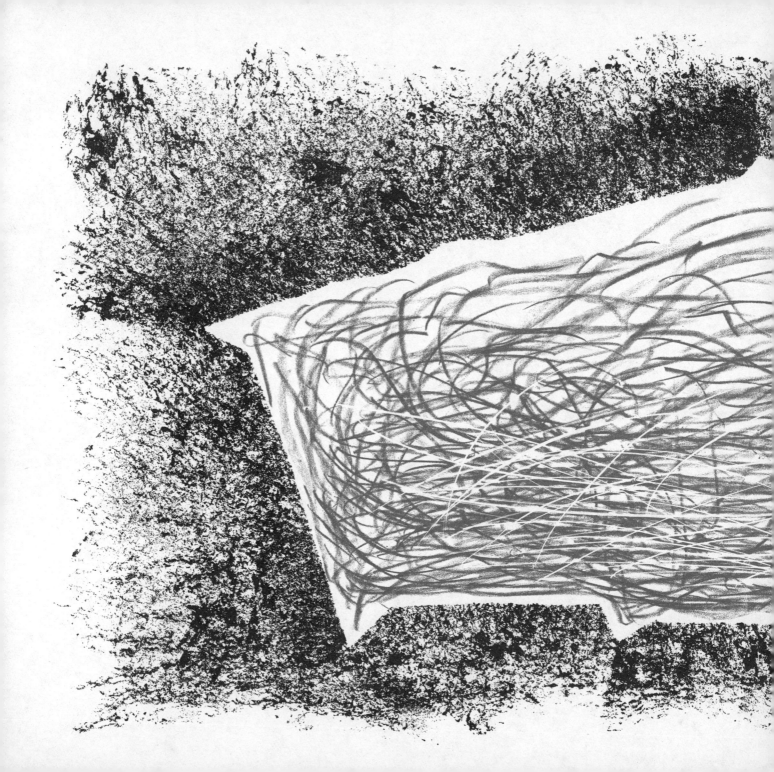

At the end of summer, a pika may have gathered
fifty pounds of grass.

He hides it under rocks.
In winter, he eats the dry grass.

It keeps him alive.

Squirrels gather food, too, and save it for winter.
They dig holes in the ground.
They bury hickory nuts and acorns.
When winter comes, they dig them up and eat them.
Sometimes squirrels forget where they buried the
nuts.
Trees may grow from the nuts that squirrels forget.

Some animals do not get ready for winter at all.
They do not store food.
They do not hibernate.
They must hunt for food all winter long.

There are mice that must hunt all winter for seeds of
goldenrod, asters, and other wild plants.
Sometimes they eat the farmer's corn, oats, and
wheat.

The deer must dig in the snow for dried leaves, plants, and moss.
When the snow is deep, he must eat the twigs, buds, and bark of trees.

The rabbit must hunt under the snow for bits of
  grass and plants.
When the snow is deep, he, too, eats buds and bark
  of bushes so he can stay alive.

In the winter the fox hunts for mice and rabbits.
So does the wolf.
When the winter is cold and the snow is deep,
many animals cannot find food.
They get very hungry.

These are some of the ways of wild animals in winter.

ABOUT THE AUTHOR

Henrietta Newman Bancroft taught nature study and elementary science at the Walden School in New York, where for many years she maintained a large nature room frequently filled with as many as twenty different kinds of animals.

Miss Bancroft received her early education in Buffalo, New York, and later attended the New York State College of Agriculture, Allegheny Nature School, and the University of Colorado. Besides traveling throughout the United States, she has visited many European countries and lived for a year in France and Switzerland.

ABOUT THE ILLUSTRATOR

Gaetano di Palma, otherwise known as "Tino," came to the United States from Italy in 1959. Several of his illustrations have appeared in such books, magazines, and newspapers as *Time, Columbia Encyclopedia, Natural History, Popular Boating,* and *The New York Times.*

He is a scientific illustrator at the American Museum of Natural History as well as a free-lance commercial artist.

Mr. di Palma is the designer of the 1964 Christmas seal for the National Tuberculosis Association. He lives in Darien, Connecticut, with his wife and two sons.